The

BANKRUPTCY

WORKBOOK

ISBN-13: 978-1466284807

Printed in the United States of America

Attorney/Firm Name

Address

City, State Zip

Office Contact Person _____

Office Contact Phone _____

Office Contact Email _____

There are 97 bankruptcy districts in the United States. Bankruptcy is guided by federal law, so much of it is the same no matter where you live. However, each of those districts have local rules and their own Trustees that oversee the process. Because of the individual quirks of each district, having an attorney with experience in that district is to your benefit. The forms used in bankruptcy are standard everywhere, yet the level of detail varies from district to district. The rule here is, disclose, disclose, disclose. Tell your attorney everything, don't hide debts or assets. Every once in a while someone tries and the vast majority of the time, they are caught. Remember, bankruptcy is FEDERAL law and violations of FEDERAL law are handled by the FBI. It is a serious business and honesty is your ONLY option. Attorneys, trustees, clerks and judges see hundreds or thousands of petitions a year, don't hide information.

Your situation is unique in the details, but not in general - you now have more debt than you can pay and there is little or no hope of that situation ever changing. In the simplest terms, bankruptcy gives you a chance to start over. This workbook will help to put together the information and documents you will need regardless of district or attorney. You will find several disclosures/notices that must be provided to you. If your attorney gave you this book, go ahead and sign and date them.

After the disclosures will be checklists and information that will help with the process. Read them carefully. You will note in some cases items have been repeated several times. This is because no matter how often an attorney or their staff repeat the information, clients seem to 'forget' them.

Finally the data sheets. Complete them to the best of your ability. Accuracy and completeness are very important. Attorneys can deal with problems they know about; finding out about assets you didn't disclose after the fact can be detrimental to your financial well being (not to mention the criminal risks). If there is a section where you need more room, attach a separate sheet.

All the work will pay off in the end. A smooth process is the goal of everyone involved, not just you! When everything works right, the most common emotion expressed by clients is

RELIEF

Disclosures

The following pages are notices the Court requires you be given immediately after hiring an attorney and prior to filing bankruptcy. If your attorney gave you this workbook, read and sign them.

Disclosure Pursuant to 11 U.S.C. §527(a)(2)

You are notified:

1.   All information that you are required to provide with a petition and thereafter during a case under the Bankruptcy Code is required to be complete, accurate, and truthful.

2.   All assets and all liabilities are required to be completely and accurately disclosed in the documents filed to commence the case. Some places in the Bankruptcy Code require that you list the replacement value of each asset. This must be the replacement value of the property at the date of filing the petition, without deducting for costs of sale or marketing, established after a reasonable inquiry. For property acquired for personal, family, or household use, replacement value means the price a retail merchant would charge for property of that kind, considering the age and condition of the property.

3.   The following information, which appears on Official Form 22, Statement of Current Monthly Income, is required to be stated after reasonable inquiry: current monthly income, the amounts specified in section 707(b)(2), and, in a case under chapter 13 of the Bankruptcy Code, disposable income (determined in accordance with section 707(b)(2)).

4.   Information that you provide during your case may be audited pursuant to provisions of the Bankruptcy Code. Failure to provide such information may result in dismissal of the case under this title or other sanction, including criminal sanctions.

Signature _____ Date _____

Spouse Signature _____ Date _____

IMPORTANT INFORMATION ABOUT BANKRUPTCY ASSISTANCE SERVICES FROM AN ATTORNEY OR BANKRUPTCY PETITION PREPARER.

If you decide to seek bankruptcy relief, you can represent yourself, you can hire an attorney to represent you, or you can get help in some localities from a bankruptcy petition preparer who is not an attorney. THE LAW REQUIRES AN ATTORNEY OR BANKRUPTCY PETITION PREPARER TO GIVE YOU A WRITTEN CONTRACT SPECIFYING WHAT THE ATTORNEY OR BANKRUPTCY PETITION PREPARER WILL DO FOR YOU AND HOW MUCH IT WILL COST. Ask to see the contract before you hire anyone.

The following information helps you understand what must be done in a routine bankruptcy case to help you evaluate how much service you need. Although bankruptcy can be complex, many cases are routine.

Before filing a bankruptcy case, either you or your attorney should analyze your eligibility for different forms of debt relief available under the Bankruptcy Code and which form of relief is most likely to be beneficial for you. Be sure you understand the relief you can obtain and its limitations. To file a bankruptcy case, documents called a Petition, Schedules and Statement of Financial Affairs, as well as in some cases a Statement of Intention need to be prepared correctly and filed with the bankruptcy court. You will have to pay a filing fee to the bankruptcy court. Once your case starts, you will have to attend the required first meeting of the creditors where you may be questioned by a court official called a 'trustee' and by creditors.

If you choose to file a chapter 7 case, you may be asked by a creditor to reaffirm a debt. You may want help deciding whether to do so. A creditor is not permitted to coerce you into reaffirming your debts.

If you choose to file a chapter 13 case in which you repay your creditors what you can afford over 3 to 5 years, you may also want help with preparing your chapter 13 plan and with the confirmation hearing on your plan which will be before a bankruptcy judge.

If you select another type of relief under the Bankruptcy Code other than chapter 7 or chapter 13, you will want to find out what should be done from someone familiar with that type of relief.

Your bankruptcy case may also involve litigation. You are generally permitted to represent yourself in litigation in bankruptcy court, but only attorneys, not bankruptcy petition preparers, can give you legal advice.

Signature _____ Date _____

Spouse Signature _____ Date _____

The following notice is required and the Trustee in your bankruptcy case will ask you if you have received it, understand it and if you have any questions.

STATEMENT OF INFORMATION REQUIRED BY 11 U.S.C. §341

INTRODUCTION

Pursuant to the Bankruptcy Reform Act of 1994, the Office of the United States Trustee, United States Department of Justice, has prepared this information sheet to help you understand some of the possible consequences of filing a bankruptcy petition under chapter 7 of the Bankruptcy Code. This information is intended to make you aware of...

(1)   the potential consequences of seeking a discharge in bankruptcy, including the effects on credit history;

(2)   the effect of receiving a discharge of debts

(3)   the effect of reaffirming a debt; and

(4)   your ability to file a petition under a different chapter of the Bankruptcy Code.

There are many other provisions of the Bankruptcy Code that may affect your situation. This information sheet contains only general principles of law and is not a substitute for legal advice. If you have questions or need further information as to how the bankruptcy laws apply to your specific case, you should consult with your lawyer.

WHAT IS A DISCHARGE?

The filing of a chapter 7 petition is designed to result in a discharge of most of the debts you listed on your bankruptcy schedules. A discharge is a court order that says you do not have to repay your debts, but there are a number of exceptions. Debts which may not be discharged in your chapter 7 case include, for example, most taxes, child support, alimony, and student loans; court-ordered fines and restitution; debts obtained through fraud or deception; and personal injury debts caused by driving while intoxicated or taking drugs. Your discharge may be denied entirely if you, for example, destroy or conceal property; destroy, conceal or falsify records; or make a false oath. Creditors cannot ask you to pay any debts which have been discharged. You can only receive a chapter 7 discharge once every eight (8) years.

WHAT ARE THE POTENTIAL EFFECTS OF A DISCHARGE?

The fact that you filed bankruptcy can appear on your credit report for as long as 10 years. Thus, filing a bankruptcy petition may affect your ability to obtain credit in the future. Also, you may not be excused from repaying any debts that were not listed on your bankruptcy schedules or that you incurred after you filed for bankruptcy.

WHAT ARE THE EFFECTS OF REAFFIRMING A DEBT?

After you file your petition, a creditor may ask you to reaffirm a certain debt or you may seek to do so on your own. Reaffirming a debt means that you sign and file with the court a legally enforceable document, which states that you promise to repay all or a portion of the debt that may otherwise have been discharged in your bankruptcy case. Reaffirmation agreements must generally be filed with the court within 60 days after the first meeting of the creditors.

Reaffirmation agreements are strictly voluntary — they are not required by the Bankruptcy Code or other state or federal law. You can voluntarily repay any debt instead of signing a reaffirmation agreement, but there may be valid reasons for wanting to reaffirm a particular debt.

Reaffirmation agreements must not impose an undue burden on you or your dependents and must be in your best interest. If you decide to sign a reaffirmation agreement, you may cancel it at any time before the court issues your discharge order <u>or</u> within sixty (60) days after the reaffirmation agreement was filed with the court, whichever is later. If you reaffirm a debt and fail to make the payments required in the reaffirmation agreement, the creditor can take action against you to recover any property that was given as security for the loan and you may remain personally liable for any remaining debt.

OTHER BANKRUPTCY OPTIONS

You have a choice in deciding what chapter of the Bankruptcy Code will best suit your needs. Even if you have already filed for relief under chapter 7, you may be eligible to convert your case to a different chapter.

Chapter 7 is the liquidation chapter of the Bankruptcy Code. Under chapter 7, a trustee is appointed to collect and sell, if economically feasible, all property you own that is not exempt from these actions.

Chapter 11 is the reorganization chapter most commonly used by businesses, but it is also available to individuals. Creditors vote on whether to accept or reject a plan, which also must be approved by the court. While the debtor normally remains in control of the assets, the court can order the appointment of a trustee to take possession and control of the business.

Chapter 12 offers bankruptcy relief to those who qualify as family farmers. Family farmers must propose a plan to repay their creditors over a three-to-five year period and it must be approved by the court. Plan payments are made through a chapter 12 trustee, who also monitors the debtor's farming operations during the pendency of the plan.

Finally, chapter 13 generally permits individuals to keep their property by repaying creditors out of their future income. Each chapter 13 debtor writes a plan which must be approved by the bankruptcy court. The debtor must pay the chapter 13 trustee the amounts set forth in their plan. Debtors receive a discharge after they complete their chapter 13 repayment plan. Chapter 13 is only available to individuals with regular income whose debts do not exceed $1,000,000 ($250,000 in unsecured debts and $750,000 in secured debts).

AGAIN, PLEASE SPEAK TO YOUR LAWYER IF YOU NEED FURTHER INFORMATION OR EXPLANATION, INCLUDING HOW THE BANKRUPTCY LAWS RELATE TO YOUR SPECIFIC CASE.

Signature _____ Date _____

Spouse Signature _____ Date _____

The following Notice will be included in your bankruptcy petition filing.

UNITED STATES BANKRUPTCY COURT

NOTICE TO INDIVIDUAL CONSUMER DEBTOR UNDER § 342(b)
OF THE BANKRUPTCY CODE

In accordance with § 342(b) of the Bankruptcy Code, this notice: (1) Describes briefly the services available from credit counseling services; (2) Describes briefly the purposes, benefits and costs of the four types of bankruptcy proceedings you may commence; and (3) Informs you about bankruptcy crimes and notifies you that the Attorney General may examine all information you supply in connection with a bankruptcy case. You are cautioned that bankruptcy law is complicated and not easily described. Thus, you may wish to seek the advice of an attorney to learn of your rights and responsibilities should you decide to file a petition. Court employees cannot give you legal advice.

1. Services Available from Credit Counseling Agencies

With limited exceptions, § 109(h) of the Bankruptcy Code requires that all individual debtors who file for bankruptcy relief on or after October 17, 2005, receive a briefing that outlines the available opportunities for credit counseling and provides assistance in performing a budget analysis. The briefing must be given within 180 days **before** the bankruptcy filing. The briefing may be provided individually or in a group (including briefings conducted by telephone or on the Internet) and must be provided by a nonprofit budget and credit counseling agency approved by the United States trustee or bankruptcy administrator. The clerk of the bankruptcy court has a list that you may consult of the approved budget and credit counseling agencies.

In addition, after filing a bankruptcy case, an individual debtor generally must complete a financial management instructional course before he or she can receive a discharge. The clerk also has a list of approved financial management instructional courses.

2. The Four Chapters of the Bankruptcy Code Available to Individual Consumer Debtors

Chapter 7: Liquidation ($245 filing fee, $75 administrative fee, $15 trustee surcharge: Total Fee $335)
1. Chapter 7 is designed for debtors in financial difficulty who do not have the ability to pay their existing debts. Debtors whose debts are primarily consumer debts are subject to a "means test" designed to determine whether the case should be permitted to proceed under chapter 7. If your income is greater than the median income for your state of residence and family size, in some cases, creditors have the right to file a motion requesting that the court dismiss your case under § 707(b) of the Code. It is up to the court to decide whether the case should be dismissed.
2. Under chapter 7, you may claim certain of your property as exempt under governing law. A trustee may have the right to take possession of and sell the remaining property that is not exempt and use the sale proceeds to pay your creditors.
3. The purpose of filing a chapter 7 case is to obtain a discharge of your existing debts. If, however, you are found to have committed certain kinds of improper conduct described in the Bankruptcy Code, the court may deny your discharge and, if it does, the purpose for which you filed the bankruptcy petition will be defeated.
4. Even if you receive a general discharge, some particular debts are not discharged under the law. Therefore, you may still be responsible for most taxes and student loans; debts incurred to pay nondischargeable taxes; domestic support and property settlement obligations; most fines, penalties,

forfeitures, and criminal restitution obligations; certain debts which are not properly listed in your bankruptcy papers; and debts for death or personal injury caused by operating a motor vehicle, vessel, or aircraft while intoxicated from alcohol or drugs. Also, if a creditor can prove that a debt arose from fraud, breach of fiduciary duty, or theft, or from a willful and malicious injury, the bankruptcy court may determine that the debt is not discharged.

Chapter 13: Repayment of All or Part of the Debts of an Individual with Regular Income ($235 filing fee, $75 administrative fee: Total fee $310)

1. Chapter 13 is designed for individuals with regular income who would like to pay all or part of their debts in installments over a period of time. You are only eligible for chapter 13 if your debts do not exceed certain dollar amounts set forth in the Bankruptcy Code.

2. Under chapter 13, you must file with the court a plan to repay your creditors all or part of the money that you owe them, using your future earnings. The period allowed by the court to repay your debts may be three years or five years, depending upon your income and other factors. The court must approve your plan before it can take effect.

3. After completing the payments under your plan, your debts are generally discharged except for domestic support obligations; most student loans; certain taxes; most criminal fines and restitution obligations; certain debts which are not properly listed in your bankruptcy papers; certain debts for acts that caused death or personal injury; and certain long term secured obligations.

Chapter 11: Reorganization ($1167 filing fee, $550 administrative fee: Total fee $1717)

Chapter 11 is designed for the reorganization of a business but is also available to consumer debtors. Its provisions are quite complicated, and any decision by an individual to file a chapter 11 petition should be reviewed with an attorney.

Chapter 12: Family Farmer or Fisherman ($200 filing fee, $75 administrative fee: Total fee $275)

Chapter 12 is designed to permit family farmers and fishermen to repay their debts over a period of time from future earnings and is similar to chapter 13. The eligibility requirements are restrictive, limiting its use to those whose income arises primarily from a family-owned farm or commercial fishing operation.

3. Bankruptcy Crimes and Availability of Bankruptcy Papers to Law Enforcement Officials

A person who knowingly and fraudulently conceals assets or makes a false oath or statement under penalty of perjury, either orally or in writing, in connection with a bankruptcy case is subject to a fine, imprisonment, or both. All information supplied by a debtor in connection with a bankruptcy case is subject to examination by the Attorney General acting through the Office of the United States Trustee, the Office of the United States Attorney, and other components and employees of the Department of Justice.

WARNING: Section 521(a)(1) of the Bankruptcy Code requires that you promptly file detailed information regarding your creditors, assets, liabilities, income, expenses and general financial condition. Your bankruptcy case may be dismissed if this information is not filed with the court within the time deadlines set by the Bankruptcy Code, the Bankruptcy Rules, and the local rules of the court.

Signature _____   Date _____

Spouse Signature _____   Date _____

How Ordering Your Credit Report Can Help You in Bankruptcy

It is recommended that potential clients obtain a credit report for the reasons listed below. If you are married, it is recommended that you obtain credit reports (if married, for both you and your spouse). A free credit report is available from **http://www.annualcreditreport.com** You will receive a printed copy of the report in the mail for your review.

1. Obtaining the credit report helps get accurate creditor names, addresses, types of debt, balances due, and account numbers.

2. Through your credit report, you may find creditors whom you have overlooked. For a debt to be discharged, it must be listed in your bankruptcy pleadings, so it's important that you find out about all debts.

3. Credit reports can alert you to judgments against you.

4. Credit reports can alert you to liens against your property, and the need to seek lien avoidance under §522(f), thus helping you protect your property in some cases.

5. You may find out about co-signers to some of your debts, which are important to list in a bankruptcy.

6. If you are married, there may be surprising items on your credit report or your spouse's, and the reports can help determine whether you should file individually or jointly.

7. You may find out about debts created by a former spouse, who may have forged your signature to obtain credit.

8. Credit reports can alert you to mistakes on your credit record. The report will list the names and addresses of all three major credit bureaus whom you can contact to correct any mistakes or provide updated information.

9. Credit reports often contain the names and addresses of collection agencies representing creditors, and notification can be sent to these collection agencies about the bankruptcy so that collection efforts stop.

10. If the IRS has a tax lien on your property, the credit report will alert you so that it can be dealt with properly.

11. Knowing what is on your credit report can help you get credit approval for important purchases after your debts are discharged.

Not every creditor reports debts to a credit bureau, so your credit report will not list all debts. You should be sure to let your attorney know about all debts you are aware of.

Documentation you will need:

1.   6 months of pay stubs from all employers. The last 60 days of pay stubs you receive before filing must be included with your petition filing.

2.   The last 3 months of credit card, auto loan, and/or mortgage loan statements.

3.   The last 6 months of checking account, savings account or other financial account statements.

4.   State and Federal tax returns and W2s for the last 2 years. If you are missing them, you can get tax and wage transcripts from the IRS, call the IRS **ASAP** at (800) 829-1040. Some districts require the transcripts even if you have the returns and W2s.

5.   Your last 6 utility bills for each utility. (or a printout from the utility showing bill and paid)

6.   Copies from the Recorder/Register of Deeds of deeds and mortgages on real estate (these must be copies of the **recorded** documents)

7.   Copies of all titles and registration on all vehicles.

8.   If you refinanced or closed on a mortgage in the last year, a copy of the closing statement

9.   Proof of insurance on home and vehicles, in many places renters insurance.

CREDIT COUNSELING and CREDIT MANAGEMENT COURSES

1.   **Credit Counseling** is required by the law prior to filing bankruptcy. You must receive a certificate from an approved service prior to filing. The certificate is only good for 180 days and if you don't file within that 180 days, you will have to retake it.

2.   Your attorney will have a list of approved agencies, or will be working with a specific one they recommend. The Agency has no connection to your Bankruptcy Attorney. It does not share any information with the Attorney and the Attorney doesn't share any information with it. These are not pass/fail or graded courses, there are no wrong answers – be truthful and accurate and the information they provide will reflect that.

3.   **Credit Management Course** must be completed AFTER you file for bankruptcy. It must be done with 45 days of your 341/First Meeting of Creditors hearing – which is held 25-35 days after you file. Failure to complete the course will result in no discharge from your bankruptcy.

4.   Both courses can be completed online or via the phone and in some places in person. The Credit Counseling will take 1.5-2 hours, the Credit Management will take about 3 hours. If you are married and filing jointly, take it together if you can, but it can be taken separately.

REMEMBER, these are mandated by the Law and are not negotiable. They MUST be completed within the time frames given.

ALL BANKRUPTCY CASES

This workbook asks for a great deal of information, complete it to the best of your ability. If you have questions about any part of it, call the office, we will be happy to answer them. The following items will help you in preparation and in the days leading up to the filing of your case. You should feel free to call whenever you have questions or concerns.

1.   The documents you need are items we must have to file your case. Read it carefully. If you do not know how to obtain the information requested, call us!

2.   If you have any type of loan, credit card, mortgage or other debt with the same bank, savings and loan or credit union (institution) that you have a checking or savings account, the institution can freeze your accounts. It is strongly suggested you move those funds out of the your current institution and open new accounts with a different institution prior to filing your case!

3.   If **ANYALING** happens that affects your ability to complete your paperwork or file your case as planned, you **MUST** contact us immediately. **DO NOT** wait until the a court notifies you of new proceedings or a creditor files a new lawsuit. There are many things we can do if we know a problem is coming.

4.   If you receive an unscheduled, large sum of money (thousands or tens of thousands of dollars), contact the office. Paying a large amount of money to creditors may not be in your best interest.

If you have any questions, **PLEASE CALL!**   We are always glad to hear from you and will do anything we can to help you succeed.   If it is going to take some time to have the funds necessary to file your case, let us know, in some cases we can offer some suggestions.

Signature _____   Date _____

Here we go! Remember, complete EVERY question and be as accurate as possible. If something does not apply MARK N/A!

Your name _____ Social security number _____

Have you used any other name(s)? List _____ Your age _____

Street Address _____ City _____ Zip _____ County _____

Mailing address if different _____

Spouse name _____ Social security number _____

Has spouse used any other names(s)? List _____ Spouse age _____

IF DIFFERENT, Spouse's

Street Address _____ City _____ Zip _____ County _____

Mailing address if different _____

If either of you have not lived at this address for the last 3 years, list each additional address and the dates you lived there

_____

_____

BUSINESS: Do you own a business? (Circle one)   YES   NO

Are you (Mark one) Sole Proprietor_____   LLC_____   S-Corp_____   C-Corp_____

Name of Business (if any) _____

Address (even if same as home) _____

City, State, ZIP _____ Phone: _____

Type of Business _____ Start Date (Month/Year) _____

If closed, end date (Month/Year) _____

BANKRUPTCY: IF you have filed for bankruptcy in the last 9 years, complete the following:

DISTRICT _____ Date filed _____

CASE # _____ Discharged ? (Circle one)   YES   NO

CREDIT COUNSELING: You must complete Credit Counseling before you file for bankruptcy   Do not take the course until you are ready to file.

-----------------ATTACH CERTIFICATES---------------

Name of Agency_____

Debtor Certificate #_____ Date completed _____

Spouse certificate #_____ Date completed _____

RESIDENCE: If you RENT your current residence, complete the following:

Landlord Name _____

Landlord Address _____ City, State Zip _____

Do you have a lease? (Circle one)   YES   NO   What date does the lease end? _____

How much is the security deposit? _____ Are you behind on your rent? (Circle one) YES   NO

-----------------ATTACH COPY OF THE LEASE-----------------

If you OWN your home, complete the following section:

Date purchased _____ Owner(s) _____

Describe the home and property (type house, # of bedrooms & bathrooms, garage, size lot)

_____

----------------ATTACH COPY OF THE DEED---------------

A valuation must be put on all real estate - if you had an appraisal done in the last year, attach it. If not, ask a Realtor to give you a written Market Appraisal for each piece of real estate. Websites such as Zillow.com can give you a rough idea and in some areas are sufficient evidence of value. Tax Assessor statements of Fair Market Value are also sometimes accepted. Check with the office.

Approximate CURRENT Value: _____

If you own the property with someone other than your spouse, complete the following:

Percentage YOU own _____% Value of YOUR share _____

--------------ATTACH COPIES OF NOTES and MORTGAGES---------------

Many districts require the Mortgage to be a copy of the recorded mortgage - in other words, the copy of the mortgage with all the signatures that was filed with the County agency that records real estate transactions, sometimes called the Recorder of Deeds. You will need to visit the agency to obtain a copy - the copy you received at closing **IS NOT A RECORDED COPY.**

First Mortgage Holder name _____

Address _____
                (use address on statement listed for correspondence)

Mortgage account # _____

Principle balance $_____ Monthly payment $_____

If you are behind on payments,

Past due balance _____ Date you made last payment _____

Does this payment include TAXES: (Circle one) YES   NO   INSURANCE: (Circle one) YES   NO

Second Mortgage Holder name _____

Address _____
                (use address on statement listed for correspondence)

Mortgage account # _____

Principle balance $_____ Monthly payment $_____

If you are behind on payments,

Past due balance _____ Date you made last payment_____

-----ATTACH COPY OF MOST RECENT MORTGAGE STATEMENT FOR ALL LOANS-----

SECOND HOME OR ANY OTHER REAL ESTATE (in whole or as a part owner), complete the following information:

Date purchased _____ Address _____

Approximate CURRENT Value _____

List ALL owners, including yourself, spouse and any others:

Owner _____ Percentage _____

Owner _____ Percentage _____

-----ATTACH COPIES OF NOTES and MORTGAGES-----

First Mortgage Holder name: _____

Address _____
       (use address on statement listed for correspondence)

Mortgage account # _____

Principle balance $_____ Monthly payment $_____

If you are behind on payments:

Past due balance _____ Date you made last payment _____

Does this payment include TAXES: (Circle one) YES   NO   INSURANCE: (Circle one) YES   NO

Second Mortgage Holder name _____

Address _____
       (use address on statement listed for correspondence)

Mortgage account # _____

Principle balance $_____ Monthly payment $_____

If you are behind on payments, _____

Past due balance _____ Date you made last payment _____

-----ATTACH COPY OF MOST RECENT MORTGAGE STATEMENT FOR ALL LOANS-----

VEHICLES: List each car, truck, motorcycle or RV, running or not that is titled in/owned by you/spouse

Year, Make Model _____ Miles on odometer _____

Names on title (Include everyone) _____

Lender Name_____ Address _____

　Acct #_____ Balance $_____ Monthly payment $_____

Are you current on this loan? (Circle one) YES NO   Do you want to keep it? (Circle one) YES NO

Year, Make Model _____ Miles on odometer _____

Lender Name_____ Address _____

　Acct #_____ Balance $_____ Monthly payment $_____

Are you current on this loan? (Circle one) YES NO   Do you want to keep it? (Circle one) YES NO

----------ATTACH CURRENT LOAN STATEMENTS FOR EACH LOAN ----------

OTHER VEHICLES: If you have a boat, jetski, snowmobile or trailer, provide the following.

Year, Make Model _____ What is it's value $ _____

Lender_____ Address _____

Acct #_____ Balance $_____ Monthly payment $_____

Are you current on this loan? (Circle one) YES NO   Do you want to keep it? (Circle one) YES NO

----------ATTACH CURRENT LOAN STATEMENTS FOR EACH LOAN ----------

PERSONAL/HOUSEHOLD GOODS **Complete each section or mark NA if appropriate – Use a good faith estimate of the value to replace with something of equal age and condition:**

Household goods - Furniture, utensils, linens/bedding: $_____

Electronics - TVs, radios, computers (not for business), digital collections (video/music), cell phones, printers: $_____

Collectibles - Books, paintings, artwork, collections, nic-nacs: $_____

Sports equipment - skis, golf clubs, camping/fishing/exercise equipment: $_____

Hobby – musical instruments, cameras, arts/crafts equipment/supplies: $_____

Guns - list type and value: $_____

Clothing – clothes, shoes, coats: $_____

Jewelry - Necklaces, earrings, bracelets, rings, costume jewelry, watches: $_____

Wedding rings: $_____ Is there an appraisal/insurance on any jewelry? Provide copy if so.

Pets, including horses – Type and number: _____

FINANCIAL ASSETS:

Cash on hand: This changes from day to day, don't worry. Wallet/Purse _____

Bank or Credit union name _____ Account # _____

List ALL names on account _____

Bank or Credit union name _____ Account #_____

List ALL names on account _____

Bank or Credit union name _____ Account # _____

List ALL names on account _____

Brokerage name _____ Account #_____

List ALL names on account _____

----------**ATTACH THE LAST 6 MONTHS OF STATEMENTS FOR EACH ACCOUNT**----------

Do you have any non-retirement annuities? List holder and value _____

Do you have an Educational or State Tuition offered annuity?

List holder and value _____

Do you have any stock, government or corporate bonds?

Type, number of shares, value_____

RETIREMENT - EMPLOYER: If you have a retirement accounts such as Pension, 401k, 457 or IRA, list the name of the employer and the company that manages such as Union Local 1 with New York Life

Type ____ Name _____ managed by _____ Balance $_____

Type ____ Name _____ managed by _____ Balance $_____

Type ____ Name _____ managed by _____ Balance $_____

---------- **ATTACH RECENT STATEMENT FOR EACH ACCOUNT** ----------

RETIREMENT – PERSONAL: If you have an PERSONAL retirement accounts such as IRA, Roth IRA

Type ____ Company Name _____ Balance $_____

Type ____ Company Name _____ Balance $_____

---------- **ATTACH RECENT STATEMENT FOR EACH ACCOUNT** ----------

Other than security deposit on residence, any other security deposits? (utility, business, service)

List each holder and amount:_____

Do you have an interest in someone else's estate? Details:

_____

Do you own any patents, copyrights, franchises? Details

_____

Do you hold any professional licenses such as RN, CPA, Real Estate? List

_____

IF YOU WILL FILE BETWEEN DECEMBER 15TH AND APRIL 30TH COMPLETE:

Anticipated Federal Refund: $_____ Anticipated State Refund: $_____

----------ATTACH STATE/FEDERAL TAX RETURNS FOR PREVIOUS TWO YEARS---------
---------INCLUDING ALL SCHEDULES, W2S and 1099s---------

Many districts require tax return transcripts from the IRS proving you have filed your returns. Transcripts can be ordered from the IRS at (800) 829-1040

INSURANCE: Provided by employer (Group Whole, Group Term, Short/Long Term Disability)

Type _____ Amount _____ Beneficiary _____ Value _____

Type _____ Amount _____ Beneficiary _____ Value _____

Type _____ Amount _____ Beneficiary _____ Value _____

INSURANCE: You purchase (Homeowners, renters, auto, life), **PROVIDE DECLARATION PAGES**

Home/Renters – Insurer_____ Policy # _____

Auto/Vehicle – Insurer _____ Policy # _____

Life insurance, list each policy, **PROVIDE DECLARATION PAGES**

Insurance company: _____ Who is insured? _____ Beneficiary? _____

Select type of policy: Term Whole Universal   Death Benefit $_____ Cash value $_____

Insurance company: _____ Who is insured? _____ Beneficiary? _____

Select type of policy: Term Whole Universal   Death Benefit $_____ Cash value $_____

Insurance company: _____ Who is insured? _____ Beneficiary? _____

Select type of policy: Term Whole Universal   Death Benefit $_____ Cash value $_____

INHERITANCE from someone that has already died:

From who_____ Proceeds(what)_____

THIRD PARTY CLAIMS: Can you sue anyone for worker's compensation or personal injury? Need details (and attorney's name if you have retained one).

_____

BUSINESS ASSETS

Do you have an interest in a corporation, partnership or joint venture other than previously listed?

List name of business, percentage owned, and value _____

Do you own an interest in business real estate or business related property? If yes, list

Address _____ Share/Ownership type _____ Value $_____

List any commissions or accounts receivable due: $_____

List any office equipment, computers, furnishings and supplies and their value _____

_____

_____

List any machinery, fixtures, equipment and tools and their value _____

_____

List any business inventory and its value and basis _____

List any customer lists, mailing lists or other compilations and their value
_____

Other assets: Anything else of value such as season tickets, club memberships and their approximate value

_____

_____

PRIORITY DEBTS

Federal Taxes Owed
Year _____ Did you file on time (Circle one) YES NO Amount owed $_____

Year _____ Did you file on time (Circle one) YES NO Amount owed $_____

Year _____ Did you file on time (Circle one) YES NO Amount owed $_____

----------ATTACH RECENT STATEMENT----------

State Taxes Owed
Year _____ State _____ Did you file on time (Circle one) YES NO Amount owed $_____

Year _____ State _____ Did you file on time (Circle one) YES NO Amount owed $_____

Year _____ State _____ Did you file on time (Circle one) YES NO Amount owed $_____

----------ATTACH RECENT STATEMENT----------

If you are under court order to pay child support/alimony, monthly amount? _____

Name of the person you pay support to _____

Address _____

List name(s) of the person(people) you pay support for _____

If you owe arrears, list the amount $_____

----------ATTACH MOST RECENT STATEMENT----------

If you owe money to former employees or restitution for crimes or to victims, advise your attorney and bring all documents to your meetings.

CO-SIGNERS If someone OTHER than your spouse is a co-debtor on any loan, list the loan and the persons name and address here. If YOU are a co-SIGNER on any loan other than your spouse, also list them here.

Lender _____ Co-Debtor name/address _____

Lender _____ Co-Debtor name/address _____

Co-signed for

Lender _____ Co-Debtor name/address _____

NON-RESIDENTIAL LEASES AND CONTRACTS

Automobile Lease: Yr, make, model of vehicle _____ Lease ends _____

Account number _____ Monthly payment _____

List company name and address _____

Cell phone Contracts

List company name _____ Account #_____

Address _____ Term ends_____

List company name _____ Account #_____

Address _____ Term ends_____

List company name _____ Account #_____

Address _____ Term ends_____

Cable/Satellite Contracts

List company name _____ Account #_____

Address _____ Term ends_____

List company name _____ Account #_____

Address _____ Term ends_____

Furnishings/Household goods Rent to Own Contracts

List item _____Company name _____

Address _____

Account #_____ Monthly payment $_____

List item _____Company name _____

Address _____

Account #_____ Monthly payment $_____

INCOME

Name of your employer _____ How long employed there _____

Address _____ Job Title _____

Spouse employer _____ How long employed there _____

Address _____ Job Title _____

-----ATTACH 6 FULL MONTHS OF PAY STUBS FOR EACH JOB
YOU HAVE HELD OVER THE LAST 7 MONTHS-----
This is non-negotiable. The Court requires the last 60 days of paystubs

For social security, retirements/pensions we need your most recent annual statements.

If you receive severance, or unemployment compensation or disability payments, the same requirements apply.

If your paystub does NOT include year to date totals, we need paystubs from January 1st. If your paystubs include deductions that are marked with codes or cryptic abbreviations, please provide a list that specifies what each deduction is for. If you are no longer employed and paystubs are not available, you MUST obtain a print-out from the employer(s) showing the date of pay, gross amount and all deductions.

If you have a second employer

Name of your employer _____ How long employed there _____

Address _____ Job Title _____

If your spouse has a second employer

Name of your employer _____ How long employed there _____

Address _____ Job Title _____

BUSINESS INCOME – PROVIDE INDIVIDUAL MONTHLY INCOME/EXPENSE REPORTS
(See Office for Form to Use)

Year to Date Gross Sales/Receipts _____

Year to Date Cost of Goods Sold _____

Year to Date Business Expenses _____

RE RENTAL INCOME – PROVIDE INDVIDUAL MONTHLY INCOME/EXPENSE REPORTS
(See Office for Form to Use)

Monthly rental income _____ Monthly property expenses _____

If you have children or dependents living with you, list them:

First name _____ Age _____ Relationship _____

First name _____ Age _____ Relationship _____

First name _____ Age _____ Relationship _____

First name _____ Age _____ Relationship _____

BUDGET – MONTHLY EXPENSES

Rent or 1st mortgage $_____ 2nd Mortgage $_____

If not in mortgage - Home insurance $_____ Property taxes $_____

Home/Rental insurance $_____ Home maintenance $_____

Electric/Gas utility $_____ Propane/Fuel oil $_____

Telephone/land line $_____ Cell phone $_____

Cable/Satelite $_____ Internet $_____ or Bundle $_____

Trash/garbage $_____ Water/Sewer $_____ Security $_____

Food $_____ Restaurant/Food away $_____

Childcare/Babysitting $_____

Clothing $_____ Laundry/Dry cleaning $_____

Personal items and services $_____ Meds/Doctor/Dentist out of pocket $_____

INSURANCE
Health*** $_____ Dental*** $_____ Life*** $_____
*** DO NOT INCLUDE amounts deducted from paychecks for employer provided benefits

Auto gas $_____ Auto insurance $_____ Other insurance $_____

Recreation, spending money $_____ Charity $_____

Past due tax payments $_____ Alimony/Support $_____

Education/Tuition $_____ Children's educational expenses $_____

Children's after school/sports expenses $_____

1st Auto loan $_____ 2nd Auto loan $_____

Other vehicle loan $_____ Auto lease $_____

Student loans $_____ Rent to own Contract $_____

Support for others $_____ Pet expenses $_____

Memberships $_____ Storage $_____ Other expenses $_____

List anything that will cause a 10% or more increase or decrease in income or expenses over the next year:

_____

_____

FINANCIAL AFFAIRS

Did you receive other income THIS YEAR from any other source?

From who/where: _____ Amount $_____ Dates paid _____

From who/where: _____ Amount $_____ Dates paid _____

Have you paid to any creditor more than $600 in the last 90 days?

Creditor: _____ Dates paid _____ Amount paid $_____

Creditor: _____ Dates paid _____ Amount paid $_____

Creditor: _____ Dates paid _____ Amount paid $_____

Did you pay child support or alimony in the last 90 days?

Paid to: _____ Dates paid _____ Amount paid $_____

Did you pay or make payments to any family member (or relative or business partner) in the last year?

Paid to: _____ Dates paid _____ Amount paid $_____

Paid to: _____ Dates paid _____ Amount paid $_____

Did you give any asset to an insider or creditor in lieu of a debt or payment in the last year?

Asset: _____ Creditor/Insider _____ Date _____

LAWSUITS: Has anyone sued you in the last year?

Name: _____ Case Number _____ Status _____

Court and address _____

Name: _____ Case Number _____ Status _____

Court and address _____

Name: _____ Case Number _____ Status _____

Court and address _____

Name: _____ Case Number _____ Status _____

Court and address _____

Has anyone repossessed or foreclosed assets or garnished wages in the last year?

Name: _____ Asset_____ Date_____ Value $_____

Name: _____ Asset_____ Date_____ Value $_____

Name: _____ Asset_____ Date_____ Value $_____

If you have given a gift to a person worth more than $600 or charity more than $600 in the past 2 years, list the person/charity and the gift/amounts:

Charity/Person _____ Address_____

 Date(s) _____ Gift/Amount given _____

Charity/Person _____ Address_____

 Date(s) _____ Gift/Amount given _____

Have you had any losses (fire, theft, damage)?

 Date _____ Amount of loss $_____ Cause _____

Was it covered by insurance? (Circle one) YES   NO   How much? $_____

Within the last year have you or anyone on your behalf pay or transfer property on your behalf to anyone you consulted about bankruptcy or filing bankruptcy? Include attorneys, petition preparers or credit counseling agencies.

Name/Firm Paid and address _____

Date _____ Amount Paid $_____ For _____

Person who paid if not you _____ Property _____

Name/Firm Paid and address _____

Date _____ Amount Paid $_____ For _____

Person who paid if not you _____ Property _____

Did you make payments to a person, firm or agency that promised to help you deal with or make payments to creditors on your behalf?

Person/Firm Paid and address _____

Date(s) _____ Amount paid $_____

Have you sold or transferred ANYTHING of value in the last 2 years? Real estate, cars, rec vehicles, etc.

Sold to_____ Address _____

Date sold _____ Value received $_____ Item sold _____

Did you transfer any property into a trust in the last 10 years? (Circle one) YES   NO

Have you closed any bank/financial accounts in the last year?

Bank/Institution _____ Address_____

Type of account _____ Date closed _____ Balance @ Closing $_____

Bank/Institution _____ Address_____

Type of account _____ Date closed _____ Balance @ Closing $_____

Do you have a safe deposit box? If yes, details:

 Bank/Institution_____ Address_____

 Contents _____

 Does anyone else have access to it? Name _____

                              Address _____

Are you holding any property that belongs to another person?

 Name of owner _____ Address _____

 Items held and value _____

UNSECURED DEBTS

Credit card company/Issuer	Account Number	Amount Owed
_____	_____	_____
_____	_____	_____
_____	_____	_____
_____	_____	_____
_____	_____	_____
_____	_____	_____
_____	_____	_____
_____	_____	_____
_____	_____	_____
_____	_____	_____
_____	_____	_____
_____	_____	_____
_____	_____	_____
_____	_____	_____
_____	_____	_____

Medical/Other Creditors	Address	Acct #	Amount Owed
_____	_____	_____	_____
_____	_____	_____	_____
_____	_____	_____	_____
_____	_____	_____	_____
_____	_____	_____	_____
_____	_____	_____	_____

FINAL QUESTIONS

Has any bank or financial institute withdrawn money from a checking, savings or brokerage account to pay a debt without your prior approval in the last 6 months?

Creditor	Creditor Address	Amount taken	Date taken
_____	_____	_____	_____

List the name of any ex-spouse you have had in the last 8 years

_____

Have you any property or control any property that has or had notice of environmental hazards from a governmental agency? If yes, list property address_____

THANK YOU! We know that it is not easy pulling all this information together, but the more complete and accurate it is, the less chance of any surprises in the process.   If you own or control anything not listed above, please use the space below to describe it.

www.ingramcontent.com/pod-product-compliance
Lightning Source LLC
Chambersburg PA
CBHW081245170526
45165CB00009B/3205